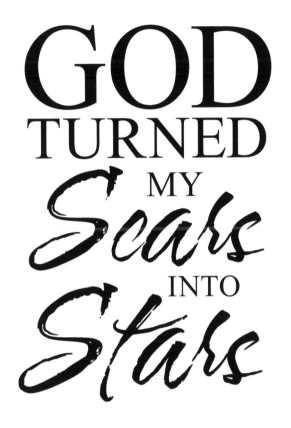

GOD
TURNED
MY
Scars
INTO
Stars

CHERYL BOYKIN - BROWN

author**HOUSE**®

AuthorHouse™
1663 Liberty Drive
Bloomington, IN 47403
www.authorhouse.com
Phone: 1 (800) 839-8640

Published by AuthorHouse 01/14/2020

ISBN: 978-1-7283-4332-7 (sc)
ISBN: 978-1-7283-4335-8 (e)

Print information available on the last page.

Scripture taken from The Holy Bible, King James Version. Public Domain

This book is printed on acid-free paper.

I dedicate this book first to God. Also, my supportive husband Calvin, my sons, Derrick, Darin and my daughter Chantel. I want to thank my children for loving me through all the rough times and believing in me. I truly thank God for my children that many days kept me going on when I wanted to give up on life but they keep me encouraged.

I also dedicate this book to my brothers, Freddie, Herman, Jasper, Willie, and Vernon who encouraged me to stay in school and get an education, in order to get a good job to take care of myself. My sisters, Linda, Angelina, Esther, and the sisters I never met Naomi and Sadie May also my brother Tiny

INTRODUCTION

My mother whose name is Esther McChern Boykins and father whose name is Fred Boykins was from Durham, North Carolina. I had 11 siblings and only three of us are still living, some of them have passed away from their destructive behavior and some because of medical reasons. My siblings were all put in foster care because of my parents' destructive behavior. My father worked as a bricklayer in Philadelphia. My mother at one time worked in Washington at the Washington DC US Mint but because of her alcoholism, she lost her job. I was born in Southwest Philadelphia, Pennsylvania at Mercy Doughlas hospital.

Dysfunctional Family Issues

One of my earliest memories is when I was six years old and my parents were consuming alcohol began to fight over monies needed to run our household and buy food. This arose because of my mother's excessive use of alcohol and spending the money. One night they were fighting and my father told my mother not to follow him up the street hollering and cursing at him. I wanted to warn my mother I saw my father put a pipe up his coat sleeve before he left the house, but it was too late she followed him up the street hollering and cursing at him. He turned around and hit her in the head with the pipe. As I stood in the doorway of our house, I hollered and cried as I saw the blood gushing from her head running down her face. My mother had a blood disorder called Hemophilia in which a person's blood cannot clot as it should and it makes it hard to stop their bleeding. My babysitter threw my little wooden chair at him hoping to slow him down but to no avail. When the ambulance workers came to take her to the hospital, they had to work tirelessly to stop the bleeding from her head. She was taken to the hospital; it resulted in her having brain trauma. I can remember her returning home with a white bandage on her head and a trach tube in her throat which allowed her to talk. The way she talked made me afraid. it was like she was a robot. Eventually, I learned to get used to her new way of talking. She had to use it for about a month. I was so young that I did not understand what was going on between my parents and why something this tragic like this would happen to my mom at the hands of my father.

This incident did not stop her from drinking. I asked her many times to please stop drinking, but I really did not understand her addiction to alcohol and the stronghold that it had on her. There was not a lot of programs for alcohol addiction in that time period as there are today. In the '60s people hid their alcohol addiction. My mom tried to hide her addiction but she started leaving me by myself and our neighbors started reporting her to the Department of Human Services. So to evade trouble with the Department of Human Services, she decided to ask a family friend to watch me, this was a big mistake because he begins to molest me this affected me mentally, physically and emotionally. This is a terrible violating ordeal for a child of my age to have gone through but deep in my heart, I knew that God was going to answer my prayer and intervene for me. This went on for a year. He also babysat a female cousin, he begins to do the same thing to her. She told her mother about what he was doing to her and the police were contacted and he went to jail; what a sigh of relief that was for me. I know that God had heard my prayers. I was overjoyed that my cousin spoke up and told the authorities about him. So that he would be put in jail, no longer to molest either of us.

Separation Anxiety

My 8th birthday was a sad one because my mother and father separated. My mother and I moved to the other side of town. I started having separation anxiety because I missed my dad a lot because when he was off of work on Sunday he would cook a good breakfast, I would wake up to the smell of Maxwell coffee perking in the pot, bacon, eggs, grits on the stove and homemade biscuits in the oven. My father did the best he knew how to keep me from becoming a ward of the state but they told him that it would not be good for him to raise me by himself since he was a male and I was a female child. To me, that did not make any sense, as long as he was taking care of me.

One good thing about the move across town was that I met my best friend, Sheila Harris. One day after school she wanted to come over my house to play, but I told her I was not allowed to have company. In reality, I was embarrassed about my living conditions. By this time my mother was so overtaken by her addiction, I had to take care of myself.

Taking Care of myself

I used a scrub board and soap to wash my clothes then hang them up in the bathroom. We did have enough money to go to the laundromat. My hair was always kept in an afro style, it was an easy way to manage it. Some of my neighbors were really nice to me, they would help me by doing my hair when I could not manage it I did the best I could to keep up my appearance so that other kids at school would not bully me, but some of them still picked fights with me. Sheila's brothers Andy, Earl, and Stevie would defend me.

My oldest brother Freddie, always stress to me the importance of education. So no matter what happened I got up every day and went to school. I held out as long as I could with not telling my best friend, Sheila about what was going on in my home. My mother would not be home a lot of times. We did not have a television nor living room furniture to sit on. We had one bed that I shared with my mother. When Sheila found out about my living situation she told me to come to her house before school to get something to eat, what a lifesaver she was to me. She did not tell her mother about my home situation yet, so she would sneak and give me some of her breakfast that her mom cooked her every morning. Her mother noticed that I was hanging around before and after school. Sheila told her about my living situation and she said that I was always welcome to their home. I began to spend the night over her house. Sheila's mom begins to treat me like one of her children, she becomes like a second mother to me,

I begin to call her mom Harris. She was a Christian and she would take me to church with her family on Sundays.

Hope in the Horizon

She talked to my mother and told her that she did not mind me coming over and spending the night with Sheila. I was so happy that I didn't have to be home alone. I learned to pray and ask God to protect me. I know that he answered my prayers. I believe that God put Sheila and her family in my life to let me know that there were still good people in the world and that everything was going to be alright.

Mom Harris wanted to adopt me but I did not was to go to school in Philadelphia, because of my previous experience of bullying.

In the year 1969 at the age of 9, my oldest brother, Freddie came to the house to let me know that mom's health was failing and the state was there to move me to a group. He told me that it was the best thing for me. Even though I could not see this to be true at that time but now, I know that it was a good decision and God once again answered my prayers. My mother and brother rode in the state car with me to the group home. The same day

I became a ward of the state because of my dysfunctional family environment. I can remember looking out the window of the car crying because I did not want to separate from my biological mother, mom Harris, Sheila, Earl, Andy or Stevie.

Complete change
of Environment

The name group home was Friend's Home for Children located in Secaane Pennsylvania. This home was historical property it was once owned by the Quakers. It was a three-story house, beautiful on the inside as well as the outside. On the outside, there was a baseball field, basketball court, and swings, plenty of land around it to run and play. On the inside, there was a recreation room with a ping pong table and other floor games for the children to play. There were shiny waxed hardwood floors throughout the first floor of the house, sparkling chandlers in the ceiling, a piano in the main living room. an eating room where the children ate meals together. The house had three floors because there was a boy's dormitory on the first floor, the second floor was a dormitory for the adolescent girls and the third floor for the teenage girls.

Every week we would have a fire drill at night in order for us to be safe in case of a fire. We kept our bedroom slippers and robe at the foot of the bed, so in case of fire, we would be prepared to run out of the house. The first time I heard the fire alarm it was in the middle of the night. The alarm scared me and I begin to cry and the house parent would sit with me until I fell back to sleep after the drill was over.

Being Taking Care Of

My childhood became more enjoyable when I placed in the children's group home is because I had the necessities needed as a female growing into adolescents. In this group home, I was also able to have my physical, mental and spiritual needs met. I loved my mom and wanted her to get better and take care of me. I was angry for a long time because of my feelings of abandonment and neglect by my parents. I would get into fights at school and at the group home. I was sent to see a psychiatrist so that I could talk about my feeling of abandonment and the other issues that bothered me. I was confused about why I was put in a group home. Therapy really helped me to cope with my abandonment issues and neglect. Also, through therapy, I learned about my anger problem and different ways to handle it. It took time for me to get through the healing process but I opened myself to the process and began to heal. I realized I had a lot of hurt and resentment inside that I did not want to deal with at the time, so it came out the wrong way. I am grateful to God for them putting me in therapy, the sessions help me to be able to talk things out and get an understanding of what and how my situation happened,

Death of Mom

In 1970, my mother passed away from alcoholism. one year after I was in the group home. The director of the group allowed me to go to the funeral home to view her body. In my mind, as I looked at her lying in the coffin, pictured she was sleeping and any moment would wake up and everything would be alright but It did not happen. She looked so beautiful in her pastel blue gown, her hair looked as if she had just come out of the beauty salon. I walked up to the casket and kissed her, knowing that it would be the last time I would see her. She looked so peaceful, all her troubles were over. I still hold that picture in my mind.

The director of the home did not think it would be a good idea for me to go to the gravesite, seeing that I was so upset and crying. I was so glad that I had mom Harris and her family in my life to help me get through this hard time.

When mom Harris found out about the death of my mother, she would come to see every chance she could and bring Sheila, Stevie, Earl, and Andy. I was so happy to see them and vice versa.

Through my years of living at the children's home. I am thankful for the Director of the home being a Christian lady. She allowed us to go to the movie to see "The Hiding Place" a movie based on the life of Corrie Ten Boom, who was a Dutch watchmaker and writer. Corrie and her family members aided Jews to escape the Nazi Holocaust during World War II by using their home to hide Jews This movie helped me to have greater gratitude for freedom because she was put in captivity by the Nazi's. Corrie was a strong Christian who had a very strong belief in Jesus Christ. Some of the lessons that I learned from this movie was:

1. Suffering gives me a greater want to live so that I can go to heaven
2. No matter what I go through it is not a reason to sin and if I do, repent to God for the sin.
3. Suffering makes one stronger and more Christlike if we submit to God daily.

This movie reminded me to forgive my debtors and not to become bitter, anger or filled with malice. Another thing I achieved from watching this moving I realized that obedience, trust, and perseverance will help me to be free of the fear of suffering. This movie helped me to understand

that being a Christian, means to look forward to the day of the return of Jesus Christ,

In the bible, it tells us "And God shall wipe away all tears from their eyes; and there shall be no more death, neither sorrow, nor crying, neither shall there be any more pain: for the former things are passed away." Revelation 21:4

My adolescent years were good because the caretakers in the

group home took good care of me. The group home caretakers were called house parents. They would make sure that each child did their chores and took care of their hygiene if we needed medicines they would administer them to us. I had an iron deficiency from being malnourished so I had to take iron pills and eat healthy to gain weight. I was put in the hospital for a week because I was to underweight and my stomach had to adjust to nutritional food.

Coming into Puberty

When I think about my experience of coming into puberty, how I wished I had my maternal mother there to show me how to take care of my personal needs but by then she had passed away. The house parents at the home explained to me what was happening in my body as I was entering into puberty. I was so scared but the house parent assured me that I would be alright and that it was a part of life as a young lady.

My foster mother, Virginia Harris sat me down and told me about hygiene. She also gives me a short sex education session. She told me that I was too young to have sex and that I had plenty of time for that later in life. Mom Harris also let me know that I could come to her any time and talk to her about anything that was on my mind. I love the relationship we had. I never felt embarrassed as I shared what was on my mind. I am so grateful to her and their other women that God put in my life beings that I did not have a mother to explain the facts of womanhood to me. These women helped me to understand that womanhood came with a lot of responsibilities.

Becoming a Teenager

When I was thirteen I was able to get my first job as a custodian in Junior High School. I enjoyed working to make money to buy the extra things that I wanted such as my own television for my room, curtains for my windows with the matching bedding, this gave me a feeling of accomplishment. I was able to open up a bank account to save money for summer camp vacation. Every week at the home the house parent would give us our weekly allowance to doing our chores and having good behavior. We also received a clothing allowance and was taken to the mall to buy the clothes that we wanted. Some of the children would get in trouble because they used their allowance to buy cigarettes. I thank God that my oldest brother broke me out of that habit before I could get started smoking cigarettes, he caught me smoking one day and make me eat some of the tobacco the taste of it make me sick to my stomach and I never wanted to smoke another cigarette. Thank God for that was a lesson well learned, I am smoke-free today.

I tried to avoid getting into trouble in the group home because we would lose our privileges. I recall the time I got into trouble for going to the mall with a group of girls from the group home and they decided to shoplift and me not thinking about the consequences of my action, I went along and did the same. We were taken to the police station and put in a holding cell until an adult came from the home to pick us up, this was a scary lesson. I was put on punishment for a month. One day the director, Mrs. Dorothy summoned me to her office to tell me that my oldest sister, Linda was in the hospital suffering from yellow jaundice, which is when cause the liver to become inflamed or the bile ducts get obstructed. One of the house parents took me to see her at the hospital. Her skin had a yellow tint to it for the infection. It really hurt that she was in this condition. I said a prayer for her quietly under my breath. Later on, I found out that my sister was living a destructive lifestyle, she had a boyfriend who abused her physically, mentally and emotionally. I was told that my father begged her to come and live with him to get away for the abuse but she declined is offer. I wanted to go and visit her when she got out of the hospital but Mrs. Dorthy said that would be a good ideal. I was really upset about the decision, so I ran away. I knew how to catch the train from traveling home with mom Harris. The conductor on the train was very nice when I asked him which bus do I need to take from the train station. His directions were very easy to follow. When I got to her house she was so surprised to see me. She asked me who allowed me to come by myself? I replied no one I ran away because I wanted to see you. She did not know if she wanted to spank me or hug me, but she chose to hug me and give me a big smile. My sister had the prettiest white teeth of anyone I knew. My sister was so nice looking and had a very warm and loving personality, I could not understand why anyone would want to abuse her this truly was beyond my understanding as was my mother's abuse. I stayed with her that night but I really didn't enjoy it because of the loud hollering between her and the boyfriend. Reminded me of my mother and father's relationship. The next day I kissed and hugged my sister good-bye then went to the train to go back to the group home.

When I got home I was put on punishment and grounded for a month. The only outing I could have was to go to church. The house parent, Ms. Anna told me that was a very dangerous thing that I had done and that anything could have happened to me on the road. Well, I never did that again.

Summer Fun

Every summer the staff would send all the boys and girls to summer camp in Sandy Cove, Maryland, where I was able to learn different activities such as horseback riding, boating, and volleyball, swimming, singing Christian songs by the campfire meeting new friends and staying in touch with them through writing letters once camp was over. I looked forward to going to camp every summer. This camp was owned by Christians, I also learned about God and how much God loves us and sent his Son Jesus to die on the cross for our sins. It was good to know that someone loved me. I was still angry about my mother leaving me at the group home. One year while I was at camp I accepted Jesus Christ into my life as my personal savior and begin to read my bible daily and pray. I asked God to help me to forgive my mother and father for the abandonment. One of the directors of the group home, Mrs. Dorhty Pepper, who was a Christian lady whose faith in God was very strong. She would always tell me that God had a plan for my life and to pray and not worry about situations in my life and that God would never leave me or forsake me. These words were very comforting but I did not want to hear what she was saying, I just wanted to go home to my family.

In September of 1975, I went to Ridley High school located in Folsom, Pennsylvania, I was 15 years old, which entitled me to invite our friends over for a visit and go to the high school dances where I would meet up with one of my closest friend Rita for social events. I was also allowed to go to her house to visit. Her mom was very nice, I enjoyed visiting with her.

Weekend Visits

Once the caseworker felt that I was ready, they allowed me to go and spend a weekend at our relative's home. My Aunt Wilma would come and pick me up on Friday and take me to her home in North Philadelphia, I would have to be back home by Sunday afternoon.

When I was sixteen years old, I met my high school sweetheart named Randy while visiting with my Aunt Wilma and my cousins. Randy was such a nice guy. He came to see me at the group home and take me out for dinner, to the mall or to music concerts, he escorted me to my high school prom we had a wonderful time.

On some weekends Mom Virginia Harris would come to the home and pick me up to visit with her. She did not drive so we would walk to the train station and get on the train to downtown Philadelphia then take a bus to her house where I would spend the weekend with my best friend Sheila and her three brothers Andy, Earl, and Steven. It was always a good visit. Mom Harris treated me just like I was her biological daughter in which I am so grateful because I learned the love of a family in which I was never shown by my own family, she would take me to the hairdresser and get my hair washed and styled. She has since passed away but I will never forget her. Sheila has passed also passed away but that is a different story for another day. My youngest brother Vernon would come some Sundays and take me to church with him. The name of the church was Paschall Deliverance Christian Church, where Reverend Annyebelle Neal was the pastor. She became someone whom I called a spiritual mother and still do today, I still stay in touch with her. I can call her for prayer for any situation and she would not hesitate to pray with me.

Aging out of the system

When I was eighteen of age, after graduating high school, the director of the group home told me that I could go to a trade school and take up a trade so that I would gain more skills to enable me to get a job when I age out of the home at age nineteen. I was so grateful for them allowing me to take up a trade.,

I decided to go to beautician school and earned my beautician license. It was 1979 when I left the group home at the age of nineteen. I really was not mentally ready to leave the group but I aged out. The world seemed to be so big once I left and got on my own. My father was still living so I went to live with him in Darby, PA. Living with him took me back to my childhood because he was still drinking but now he is getting older. He was in his sixties by now. I dislike the fact that I had to go back to that atmosphere but I had just left the group home and had nowhere else to go. Growing up I did not know too much about my siblings because we were all separated because of my mother's addiction. We did not get to see one another too often. They were all placed in different foster homes where some of them were treated badly. I was the only one who lived in a good group home. The group home that I was placed in had friendlier staff members who were not allowed to beat us. They would tell us to go sit on a chair in our room and stay there until we learned to behave. After aging out of the group home is when I met some of my brothers and sisters. When we finally got together, they would say that I was treated like the favorite child of my parents because I was put in a better group home and was able to go to school and get my high school diploma. My brothers and sister were mistreated in the foster home that they were placed in. I did not understand why they were angry at me because of this. Some of my siblings dropped out of school. I let them know that it was not my choice that it happened in the way that it did. It was not an easy adjustment for me being taken from my parents.

Adult Responsibilities

One evening my father wanted me to cut up a chicken to fry. I felt so inadequate because in the home we did not have to cook or do laundry, we had a cook and a person that washed our laundry. My boyfriend Randy showed me how to cut up the chicken. Randy and dated for six years.

I begin to look for jobs, a beauty shop in the neighborhood was hiring so I applied for a job as a shampoo girl but the chemicals that I worked with begin to affect my lungs, so I quit the job. I went to a job agency that trained me to become a receptionist. I wanted to earn enough money to get an apartment. I went to work for the National Forest Service as a receptionist in Broomall, PA. I also had a part-time job at McDonald's restaurant. Finally, I earned enough to get an apartment and some furniture. I was able to rent an apartment upstairs in the same building as my father. January of 1980, my father received a call that my sister Linda was murder by her boyfriend. She was found in the bath in a poodle of blood, my family was so devasted. My father told me that he needed me to go to the funeral parlor to get her body ready for burial. I was so uneasy with this ideal I told him I was not ready to see my sister lying in a mortuary to see a sister or to get her ready for burial. I asked him to call one of the other siblings but he said was the most reliable one to do it. This was a huge responsibility for someone who lived in a group home. I went and talked to Pastor Annyebelle about burial procedures and she gives me some advice also some of the members from the church went to the funeral parlor with me to help get what she needed for burial. Ms. Marlene One of the members suggested that I press and curl her hair but I was too upset. see my self doing it. She did it for me. After her burial was over, I begin to think about her children who are Lisa, Marlene, Nichole, and Dawn, I thought, how devasted it was for them to be without their mother. In my mind, I thought that my sister was so selfish, not to realize that she was leaving behind four beautiful girls and other family members that would miss her so much. I had to really pray that God would help me to forgive her for not listening to my father and leaving her abuser.

My Very Own Family

It was 1980 when I met my first husband, Darin, I met him going to work on the bus. He was a handsome looking and he held a good conversation. He worked in a building behind the one I worked in. Darin asked me to out on a date and we started dating, two years later I was pregnant with mu first son, Darin II. We decided to get married one year later. My wedding was not a very big one. We really loved each other and our new baby. He was such a good provider. He told me that he was looking for a house for us to move into in Southwest Philadelphia, I was so happy about the move to our new home. He did not want me to work, he told me to stay home and take care of our baby. Two years later, we had another baby and his name is Derrick. My husband was an engineer, he really enjoyed his job. On his job, he designed a patent for a gas stove and the company did not want to give him the credit for the design and ort his name on it. My husband was very upset about it and decided to ask his boss why he was not given the credit for his patent of the stove. His boss told him that he didn't have to honor his wishes and then fired him. This action was so devastating for my husband because he felt as though the company denied him the right of his own patent. My husband was a hard worker and a dedicated worker. This action was a big blow to his ego and this was the beginning of our marriage problems.

He began to get very depressed and distracted. I decided that I would go to work at a department store not too far from the house in order to help pay the bills. He went to work with his father doing construction work, building homes. He did not get along with his father too well. My husband would work for his father but his father always had in excuse about paying him.

God Will See Me Through the Storm

One day in 1986, I came home from work and found a note from my husband, that read "the children were still with the baby sitter and that he could not take the pressure of being a husband and a father" I was so devastated. I thought to myself "where did I go wrong"? I was blaming myself for the break up of my marriage. I did not know what to do. I called my pastor for prayer, she gave me so words of encouragement but I could not stop crying. Felt like the bottom had fallen from under my feet. I went and picked the children up from the babysitter and let her know what had happened. She was so surprised by my husband's actions. I was not making enough to pay the bill by myself so I decided to go to look for a shelter to live in. I remember taking the children with me to look at a shelter in Chester, PA. I remember walking out of that shelter and crying on my way back to the bus stop. I cried out to God, remembering the words of

King David in the bible said, "I was young but now I am old, never have I seen the righteous forsaken or his seeds begging for bread". The next day my pastor Reverend Annyebelle called me and told me that the church had an apartment of rent and that I welcome to rent it. She even gave me a job at the church daycare center that helped me to pay my rent. I had to get on public assistance to be able to buy food for my children. I was so happy. God is good, he did not let me down.

I decided to enroll in a technical school to become a secretary and received my Associate's degree in Secretarial. Which help me to get my first government job with the Army Recruiting Battalion in Philadelphia, PA.

Staying Hopeful

In 1987 my father was diagnosed with lung cancer. He decided to give me a down payment on a house that was located in Darby, PA. He wanted to assure that when he passed away I would have a place to live for me and the children. This was a big step for me because I knew that owning a home comes with a lot of responsibility. I was a single parent raising two children and taking care of my father who also moved in with us. Even though I did not think I could manage all of these responsibilities, I prayed about it and gave it a chance. I was so proud that I was going to be a homeowner at the age of twenty-two. In 1988 my father went to the doctor and they told him that his cancer was in remission. We were so happy. I knew that I needed to learn how to drive so I could get around easier with the children and taking my father to the doctors. I asked my youngest brother, Vernon to teach me to drive and he went with me to buy my first car. It was a 1980 yellow hack back Plymouth horizon. My youngest brother, Vernon taught me how to drive in which I am so grateful to him.

My car was not good up to driving standards in order for me to take the driver's test. When I took my driving test my co-worker named Vernetta came from Jersey to allow me to use her car to take the test because her car was more reliable. I pass the test the first time. In 1991 my father went to the doctors and he was told that his lung cancer had come back and he started to get ill. By now my father was eighty years old. This situation was difficult for me to handle.

On My Own Once Again

The boys started asking about their father and wanting to get in touch with him. I was able to get in touch with him through one of his brothers. He started coming around on the weekend to pick the boys up for the weekend. I found out that he was living with another woman with children in another state. I took my husband to court to get child support for the children. He was really angry with me for doing this but I needed him to take care of his responsibility as a father, after all, he was taking care of some other woman's children why should my children be neglected. I was hurt about my husband leaving us but in my heart, I still loved him. In 1991, my husband said that he wanted to get his life back on track and come back home. I thought it would be a good idea because the boys needed their father. So, I allowed him to come back home.

Everything was going well until one day I went to doctors and found out that I was pregnant with my third child. Knowing this, made me nervous because I did not know how it would make my husband was going to act to this news. There was so much going on in my life I decided to go to church every Sunday to get spiritual strength from serving God, without God I knew it would have impossible to go through my trials and tribulations. One evening I decided to tell my husband about my pregnancy and he became very upset. He told me to get an abortion, I was shocked at that response from him. I was two months into the pregnancy. I can remember standing at the top of the stairs and I said, "the only way that I will get rid of this baby is that you would have to push me down these stairs". Thank God he did not take me up on my crazy suggestion. He replied to me "either you get rid of the baby or I will leave. I told him to "let the doorknob him where the good Lord split him". Once again, he decided to leave. He stayed in touch with the boys. He would come by the house and drop off groceries for us. This left me to go through this pregnancy without his support but I made up in my mind that I was going have my baby with or without him. This was a difficult pregnancy but I prayed and asked God to help me to handle everything I was going through. I was still working for the Army, going to work every day enable to pay my bills. My father was getting sicker and I needed someone to watch him while I work. The children were in school during the day and afterward, they went to my neighbor's house after school.

My sister Esther decided to take him over her house until I could earn enough sick leave saved up on my job to be able to stay home with him.

The Big Challenge

In October 1992, it was time for the baby to be born. I was so afraid because I knew that I wouldn't have anyone in the delivery room with me for support and when I had the boys my husband was there. This delivery came with complications, the baby's umbilical cord was wrapped around her neck and she was choking. I asked God to protect me and my baby. The doctor told me that she would have to do an emergency C section birth. They had already prepped me for regular childbirth giving me an epidural that numbered me for the waist down. The C section was being done from above the waist and my body was not prepped for it. The doctor told me that I would feel what they would be doing to me during the delivery. She was right, I felt the cutting of my stomach and the pulling of my skin during the delivery of the baby. When she came out they immediately removed the cord from her neck, then put me under anesthesia because the pain was unbearable. I was so grateful the doctor was able to save me and my baby girl. Her brothers name her Chantel Elisha. They were so happy about their baby sister. Three days later we were allowed to go home. I was able to take three weeks off from my job using maternity leave.

My father was still at my sister's house in Southwest Philadelphia. He said wanted to come back to live with me. We were glad to have him back with us. He enough the children.

My father was so happy to see his new granddaughter. He was so happy to be able to hold her, she was only five pounds, he could hold her in one of his hands there was rather big. He told me to make sure that this would be the last baby and to take care of myself because he would not be around much longer to help me financially. This brought tears to my eyes but I knew it was true. He was still mobile at the time, so he could watch the boys when they came home from school until I came home from work.

Taking care of three children and a sick father was a difficult job but I had to do it. My sisters Esther and Angelina came over to help me and the hospice nurses came to visit with him. He was still able to walk around. My two boys Darin and Derrick was a lot of help taking care of their baby sister. When it was time to go back to work it was snowing and Icy outside, I slipped and broke my leg, what a bummer. I called my job to let them know that I would be out another six weeks. This was truly a rough time, trying to take care of a baby with a broken leg. Through faith, prayer and the strength of God, I was able to do it. Thank God for the boys they help me when I needed them to go up and down the stairs for me.

I decided to get a divorce from my husband, on the grounds of decretion. He was able to continue to see the children because I knew that it was important to them.

Going Back to Work

By the end of the year, he was in hospice care because his cancer was advancing.

When it was time to go back to work, I ask my neighbor Rosie, if she could watch him during the day until I could make arrangements with my job to take family leave in order to take care of him myself. She did not hesitate to say she would do this for me. My father loved the Word of God, he would get her to read Psalms 23 to him. He really was thankful for her looking in on him, ensuring that everything was alright. She had small children of her own, but she made a sacrifice for me.

With all that was going on in my life, my friends Amanda, Lettie and Nee Nee were also supportive of me. When I need someone to talk to they were there for me and the children, I could go to their house with the children and they would have dinner for them.

My father passed away in 1993. I felt like my world had come to an end. I truly loved my father no matter how he lived his life.

I begin to miss him so much. I begin to hang out with friends that encouraged me to start drinking alcohol. I did not let a lot of people know that I had begun to drink alcohol. I was what some would call a closet drinker. I handled my drinking responsibly by only drinking on the weekends.

I begin to use alcohol as a way to ease my pain of losing my father. I begin to date guys that were abusive to me. One guy that told me that if I left him that he would kill me. He met me one day coming out of my house taking my daughter to the babysitters and stick a knife to my side and told me that he was going to kill me. I began to pray hard asking God to be with me. I feared for my life but somehow I convinced him to throw the knife down the street drainage system and I would not tell the police what he had done. He began to cry and tell me how much I and the children meant to him. I realized that he was not mentally stable and I told him that our relationship was not what I needed. He stopped coming around. I begin to drink more often after this incident. Two years had gone by and I still missed my father terribly. I missed him telling me about the different stories about the family and going on trips down south with him.

Making a Big Move

In 1998, my job was relocating from Philadelphia, PA to Lakehurst New Jersey. I decided to keep my job and move with them. I made preparation to sell the house. It became too difficult trying to rent the house in Pennsylvania and pay for an apartment I let the house go back to the bank.

My job moved on the Naval Air Station, the landmark where the Hindenburg, a German passenger airship caught fire was destroyed on May 6, 1937, when it was attempting to dock. Moving to Jersey was a culture shock for me, I was not accustomed to driving all the time. In the area I lived, you have to drive everywhere because the public transportation system does not run like the Philadelphia transit system. It took time to adjust to my new situation of living in New Jersey.

The boys wanted to go in stay with their father while my daughter and I moved to New Jersey and found an apartment to live in. It was such a short notice of the move to New Jersey I did not have a place to live so the Army put us in a hotel and my household goods in storage. I met a girlfriend named Mary and I asked her mother could she watch my daughter for me while I worked. Ms. Robinson was such a sweet lady, she told me that she would. My daughter started calling her grandmom. I called her mom, we became like family to them. I was so glad to found new friends. That treated us like family.

Two years later, Mom Harris was diagnosed with rear blood cancer, six months later she passed away. I went back to Philadelphia to her funeral. It was such a sad occasion but I was glad to see Sheila, Stevie, Andy and Steve once again, it had been such a long time before seeing them. I really missed talking to mom Harris on the phone. She always was there to help me solve my situation.

It took a long time before I could find me and the children an apartment. We finally find an apartment. Two years later, My foster sister, Sheila, her boyfriend and her daughter Mecca was killed in a home invasion. This really took an emotional, mental, and physical effect on me. At the time I begin to consume alcohol more than usual. A friend told me to go to the church for support to get through this tragedy I decided to take the advice. The preacher that was there at the time, asked me why did I come to that particular church and to go to the church down from my house. I really felt let down by the church that is supposed to be there for people that needed to be emotionally, spiritually healed. I left that church office in tears but I called one of the church members and let them know what was said to me. She told me not to give up and to find another church, but not to continue to consume alcohol to cover up my feelings, but to go to Alcoholics Anonymous to get some help before I destroyed my life. I decided to go to the rooms of Alcoholics Anonymous, so that I could talk about what was going on in my life and to find a better way to deal with my pain. I felt good about this decision because I found the support that I needed to get through the death of my family members.

I still felt so alone and I decided to try to get some counseling. I was referred to a holistic counselor by the name of Michele. I am so glad I was able to get some counseling over the phone. She helped me to realize that all that happened in my childhood was not my fault and that I had the power as an adult to protect myself. I also talked to my childhood pastor Reverend Neal and I told what was told to me at the church I wanted to join. She told me that I needed to pray about it because of my issues of abandonment as a child, so she prayed with me. It was in the year 2004 and I have not had a drink of alcohol since. I felt so free from the bondage of Alcoholism. I praise and thank God for his deliverance from that bondage.

Turning Over a New Leaf

I am so happy that I did the footwork to get my life back in order and take care of myself. I realized that if I kept drinking I would have left my children alone without a mother. I did not like the feeling of being motherless and did not want to do this to my children. I find a church that I enjoyed attending and became a member and was ordained as an Evangelist in 2010. I also meet my loving husband and we got married in 2010. These years since I been alcohol-free has been the best years of my life. I have been living my best life. I graduated from college with my Master's Degree in Human Services Counseling: Life Coaching. I am so grateful to God that I did not allow the trials and tribulations make me want to give up and go sit and have a petty party for myself, but I took life one day at a time, cried sometimes, hollered some times but I am still here praising and worshipping God today.

In 2019 I decided to retire from working and start traveling and doing the things in life that I have not been able to do because of working most of my life and taking care of my children. I do have a part-time job, working with underprivileged children because I want to give back what was given to me as a child in the care of the state. I want to let them know that I am a survivor of the state system and they can also be a survivor. The children of today are different than in my time of growing up. They have so many challenges and so much peer pressure. I pray for them daily.

ABOUT THE AUTHOR

Mrs. Cheryl Brown was born on October 7, 1959, in Philadelphia, Pennsylvania. She graduated from Ridley High School in 1978. Evangelist Brown attended the National Education Center, in Philadelphia, Pennsylvania where she earned her Associates Degree in Secretarial Science in 1989. She has been working for the United States Army Mid-Atlantic Recruiting Battalion in Lakehurst, NJ, since 1989. Mrs. Cheryl Brown has earned her Bachelor's Degree in Psychology/Christian Counseling and her Master's Degree in Human Services/Holistic Counseling. Mrs. Cheryl Brown is married to Calvin Brown and has three children, Darin, Derrick, and Chantel Swain. She is now retired from her government job but continues to reach out to underprivileged youths.

Mrs. Cheryl Brown received Jesus Christ as her personal savior in 1970. The Lord led Mrs. Cheryl Brown to churches founded on the Word and the Cross of Jesus Christ. With assistance from anointed leaders of the Body of Christ, she grew in her relationship with the Lord. God delivered her from her own addictive behaviors and strongholds in 2004. This deliverance and intimate relationship are the basis for the passion Christ has given her to create a thirst for him while helping others that she comes in contact with in daily life.

But they that wait upon the LORD shall renew their strength; they shall mount up with wings as eagles; they shall run, and not be weary; and they shall walk, and not faint.

ISAIAH 40:31

Printed in the United States
By Bookmasters